MW01289697

Nana's Sunday Dance

Copyright © 2010, 2011 by Fay Picardi
Second Edition 2011
ISBN-13: 978-1461051251
ISBN-10: 1461051258

Some of the poems in *Nana's Sunday Dance* were pub-
lished in the following journals: *The Driftwood, Jabber-
wock, The Journal of Kentucky Studies, Kalliope, Potomac
Review, The Pen Woman* and *Transformations: A Creative
Convergence of Poets and Artists.*

Cover photograph by the author:
Grandmother Richardson's watch and glasses.
Nana Hardy's wedding ring and mourning veil.
Mother Richardson's wedding gloves and trousseau gown.
The poet's ivory bracelet and her 70th birthday rose.

Nana's Sunday Dance

Poems by
Fay Picardi

Burnt Umber Press

For my friend ... [handwritten inscription] at ... Cabrillo College,

I hope you enjoy the dance!

Fay Richardson Picardi

4/18/2012

For grandmothers, mothers and children everywhere.

Quilting from the Outside... In

Our grandmothers' quilts
    theirs lives
        and those before them
            repeat their stories.

Tell me a story
    of shimmering shale
        of millenniums condensed
            into desire.

Tell me a story
    of clear cold run of creek
        of wood and stone honed
            into a lover's touch.

Tell me a story
    of soft roundings of ridge
        of mist and fog coaxed
            into glow and dream.

Tell me a story
    and then
        and then

I will be wise
I will be calm
I will be
    a hammered dulcimer
        a haunting piece
            born of sweet resonance.

Table of Contents

Grandmothers

Nana's Sunday Dance

A Sestina

Hands on hips, she spots her hapless fowl,
her stance so seasoned in ancestral blood
she does not think of roles she needs to fill.
My Nana dresses in her dreams, so wears
the fragile gown she stitched and wore to dance
that ancient waltz which ends all girlhood flings.

Unfazed, she grabs a startled neck and flings
it round. Above her head, the circling fowl;
below, a whirling dervish winds her dance
until she holds a single, small and blood-
less head, a hidden face that wears
a mask already set, its task fulfilled.

The frantic body searches, unfulfilled,
to find its missing part, and, desperate, flings
its headless mass in constant motion, wears
out all its force. Here is a robust fowl
who paints the trees in jerks and fits of blood,
who spins about in a macabre dance.

This fenced-in world could conjure Pollock's dance
with mop and bucket, slinging paint to fill
his need. Here, one hen jettisons her blood
from tree to bush, and over budding roses flings
a random spray that never can turn fowl
again, but turns that dire shade no flower wears.

So Nana's quickly ended waltz through blood-
line passes down just as the gown she wore,
her wedding veil and gloves, the quilt that flings
its echoes from the past. Hers is the dance
our mothers, fathers knew. It helped them fill
their simple needs; first peace, then prayer, last fowl.

Quiet now, their blood, my Nana's and her fowl's.
But that fierce will her image wears, still fills
our blood, and we, too, fling our arms in dance.

Talking to the Ancestors

Sometimes before I even notice,
I am standing at the foot of the hill,
Fletcher Chapel Cemetery, listening.

They are all there, telling their stories;
father, grandmother, great-grandmother,
right up the hill of oaks to 1793.

But what I wanted to tell you about
is how Aunt Eloise came back from the dead,
a Tuesday night, so strong she took my breath away.

She came back with *Uncle Cedric*,
an old family portrait, an unexpected gift,
a testimony to other times.

Some would say it was coincidence
that Cedric came to me after all these years,
but I know it was will, her will.

Some would say it means nothing
that note she had tacked to the back
of the canvas spoke directly to me.

The scientists are wrong about spirits,
trying to pass off photos of ephemeral forms,
white and gliding silently down hallways.

Not so Aunt Eloise.

She is always surprising someone,
shimmering toward them in a fluttering of fuchsia silk,
in each hand, a clattering of silver spoons.

Architectural Genealogy

Might as well have been Tibet—
the snow, the wind whistling round,
and the midwife too far to come.

The earth still falls away
on all sides of this mountaintop,
this mound where my grandfather was born,
room of log, bed of branches.

Eight babies, one at a time, one at a time,
erupt through the screams of three young wives,
one after another laid out in the same chestnut

bed, the faint sounds of lullabies floating
over each quiet quilt in turn, then down the hill
to where the sun still casts its story
shadows onto the road.

Father to son, father to son, father to son,
until my brother reclaims from its shroud of time,
another cabin, another gathering place.

Strip it back, strip it back,
strip it back to its very ghost of the past,
hand hewn and holding
bits and pieces of other lives.

Watch and listen for signs.

Another time, another place.
The same wide planks of chestnut.
The same tracking sun.

From Scratch

Grandmother made everything from scratch.
Biscuits, yeast rolls, cakes.
"Only the best ingredients," she'd say,
"Getting it right takes time and care."

Fog rising off the Virginia mountains,
mist over Dunlap Creek,
steam from her pancakes filling the tiny room,
they are all one memory now.

It seems we were always
coming around a bend
through a tunnel, blowing the horn,
trying to see in front of us,
how to make it through the fog.

Two Miles East of Christmas

There is something about a traveling man.
Some kind of mystery you can
read in his wife's eyes when she looks
at him and sees beyond
as if he were not really there.

Grandmother had that look, waiting
while she was still young, wanting
what she could not have,
scouring dishes and clothes, and cooking
for a man who wasn't there.

He'd been a fireman, mostly,
Huntington to Lynchburg,
but his gold watch said "Engineer,"
and so did the way he walked his land:
Panama hat in summer; in winter, fine gray felt.

"There's no place I can't go
in my mind," Granddaddy used to say,
standing by the window of his hotel room
years later, an old man, listening for the 12:20.
He was the one waiting then.

I know what waiting is, and wanting
what I cannot have, pulse racing for the wrong
reason. I cannot be the woman my grandmother was,
cannot find solace in cleaning—dishes or clothes—and
always living as if my man were dead.

I love that traveling feeling,
the drone of engines, the run of the road
under the car. Nights alone, I dream of landscapes,
but I listen always, as my grandmother did,
for the distant sound of a train.

Spring Cleaning

Just a hint of pink
on the Japanese cherry tree
and Nana would declare
spring cleaning.

She would start with vinegar
and open windows,
bringing up from the garden
the rich smell of decay
which promises new growth.

She'd finish well before Memorial Day,
when she left us to go to Grayson
on the bus, her suitcase packed
with rayons and lace,
like a trousseau packed tenderly
by a bride going to meet her groom,
and hers buried those forty years
on a sunny hillside.

Just a hint of spring
and I, too, begin spring cleaning,
each year searching amid the clutter
in drawers and under beds,
for the legacy she left
of patience, calm, and will,
these forty years ago.

Stretching Curtains

Lace curtains must,
according to ancestral law,
be washed and stretched each spring,
two to a frame—readied for hanging
and the filtering of summer light.

Midmorning we'd gather,
sisters, mothers, grandmothers,
carrying bundles of wet lace, carefully
like porcelain vases;
bringing stretchers from the attic.

I dreamed we were dancing
in a Mondrian sculpture garden,
woodstrip frames everywhere
like paintings leaning against the trees
flowering all over the backyard.

Forcing the threads over the rusty nails,
my sister and I would prick our fingers,
not just once, but enough
to return us every few seconds
and firmly, from our sleepiness.

"Never mind," Nana used to say,
as we tried to stop the blood from staining.
"The secret is in the stretching."

Mothers

Eating Well

After "Mountain Family at Supper" Kentucky, 1937
M. Marvin Patterson, Black and White Photograph.
National Women's Museum for the Arts

Only one room here. Walls covered
with newspapers and tacked—
a few holes where the light comes in.
For the table, an oilcloth, threadbare and stained.

A mother myself now, I can understand
why this mother looks away,
feedsack dress and hand-me-down sweater,
five children, a husband, and watery soup for the table.

I can never leave Kentucky.
Today I am there as if I have always
been, seeing as I have
a memory in black and white.

I know these children, have played
with them in tobacco and sugar cane.
They have no curves to ease the climb,
just surge rock straight up, gully washed.

No smooth place for feet. And floorboards
set on rocks, teetering like newborn calves.
But these children are not teetering, not
tethered. They look straight at the camera.

These children are sugar cane
warriors, ready for any fight,
jousting in any dusty field, returning
from every battle, covered with victory.

Tuesday's Child

Sam Burgess' wife had her picture taken
in a rented casket, just like she was dead.
Said her husband was going to kill her anyway.
Traveled clear to Carrollton on a bus
because Joe Simpler's Home wouldn't do it.
A white suit, bleached out from green, on her lap.

She made them put paper lilies on her chest,
and powder her face real light.
Nothing would do her but a pink-lined one,
colored like the baby shoe she stole
from the family where she ironed summers.
Everybody thought that shoe was hers.

Sam Burgess' wife had the picture tinted
rose and set it in a black metal frame, a throw-away
with cracked glass from behind Clem's store.
She hung it at the foot of the cot where she slept
and watched it all day long on her days off.
Told strangers it was her daughter.

On Sundays she prayed for her soul. Then,
just like in the stories, they didn't find her
until spring, stretched out there clasping those rags
and staring at that picture. The only color about
her was the dirt under her fingernails
and the pink chenille robe she was lying on.

Picking Peaches

Danger made the mornings sharp.
Suspended between top rung and earth,
hidden midair in a cave of shadows,
I smelled ripeness and promise,
a sweetness I could taste.

On the rungs of my ladder, an ancient history
settled with the morning mist; the ghosts
of Roman Senators reclining on their silk settees,
of spice merchants arriving in caravans
(how a perfume intoxicates!), all melding

with departing ghosts from the farmhouse,
where Grandma still rocks her baby
at midnight, where the town doctor tries again
to save old man Bray (who still roams the orchard
in moonlight) from the day his gall broke.

Such small promise, these peaches
I pick today at the supermarket.
(*Assassin light!*)
I am appalled by their pallor,
by flesh so cold, smell so sterile.

Even so, I peel and slice,
sugar and wait.

Informal Education

Milton Cross, Jr. didn't bring his arm back
from the war. Years later, he told somebody
he left it on a truck bed north of Paris.
Wouldn't have another one.

His momma said Milton lost that arm
in a car accident over there. His best friend, too.
Bits and pieces flying everywhere, before they took
him away on a stretcher, crying like a baby.

Milton never went to church after that;
just worked in the store and let the preacher
come by from time to time to take him
to the sanitarium over in Louisville.

He used to drink raw turpentine,
my Daddy told me, so he could pass out
fast, fifteen minutes. But I've been out there
when it went   real   slow.

Milton would sit on the porch, rocking
that stub and drinking from a pint.
After a while the cursing started, and his wife
would have to brace her skinny arms up
against the door frame to keep him from the kids.

The boy's an engineer now, and the girl
got to be a nurse before his liver gave out.
His wife's stopped smoking, filled out some,
and married a man over in Carrolton
It's just, she don't laugh like she used to.

Parent's Day

Standing here in my kitchen,
early morning, you extended your hands
to each other for a handshake,
friendly and smiling
like strangers.

Half a century ago,
you were young lovers, never dreaming
one day a world would separate
you so in distance,
more in mind.

Together again
for a few minutes,
you are almost the same,
slipping easily into, and out of,
old patterns.

I watch you, now, inhabit
a merry-go-round of kitchens,
one table scene blurring into another,
round and round,
until the music stops,
and I stand here
still trying to hum the tune.

Red Plastic Hearts

"I want to move back.
It's not as cluttered there," she said, knowing
full well she had taken the clutter
with her when she left.

Empty ceramic pots; bunnies, pumpkins,
Santa mugs. Birthday balloons.
Ragged ribbons on wooden sticks,
red plastic hearts that say "I love you."

Old ladies take comfort in touching
old memories; seeing the remains of love,
like some great civilization,
lying about them in ruins.

What to say. How to say.
"Get rid of the clutter;
throw out the junk," knowing
looks can be deceiving.

Forsythia

She appeared with the first spring warmth,
and stood, holding a crumpled old newspaper
straight out toward me, like a child offering her mother
the first drawing she had ever made at school.
"For your garden," she pronounced in the same tone
as "Eat your carrots. Children are starving in China."

From her hand, five dark stems stretched skyward,
their nodules pregnant with greens and yellows
so pure Georgia O'Keefe would have been envious.
Beneath her fistful of soggy paper, frail roots spread out
forming parchment-colored family trees,
as she waited on the driveway, never flinching in the sun.

Where I put those stems, I no longer remember,
or if I even said thank you. Those were the busy years.

She waited twenty years before she spoke of that day.
Miles from Virginia, the two of us were watching the sun
playing outside the window of her hospital room,
bouncing its morning yellow off the Florida Sago palms.
"Reminds me of the forsythia I brought you
from home," she said simply, waiting for a response.

My mother would not retreat into her labored breathing.
She had fed children in China. She had taught students
to read in Haiti, in Sri Lanka, in Costa Rica.
She had learned the value of an amulet;
why a pioneer woman would shelter seeds

across the dessert, at any cost, carrying a bit of home
to protect her children against the wilderness.

She would stay long enough to plant her forsythia.
She would plant it in my heart,
where its roots are still spreading.

What We Know of Plenty

How we envy the rainmakers,
seeding the clouds against a drought,
bringing the rain, subduing the dust,
trying to save the crops.

In Roussillon, France,
my friends and I battled the dust.
We tackled ledges and craters,
raising red powder with every step.
Raw umber, yellow ocher, burnt sienna
covered our shoes, our clothing,
filtered into our imaginations.

For ages, artists have found color there,
ignited by the evening sun, pigment
plenty for any wall, any palette;
plenty for mystery, the caves of Lascaux.

The priest says we have no need
of plenty, wonder is enough.
The voices of lovers after love.
A pregnant bud, erupting
along the stem of some old plant.
The tender bulge of flesh
that rings the wrist of every infant,
and separates the baby from the child.

We cannot seed the world for our children,
disappearing down the road, around the bend.
We are helpless before the drought.

But we can call after them,
as our parents called after us,
"May you have enough."

Children

Pentimento

When Papa Pettijohn came back from hunting
early mornings,
we'd hear the dogs first,
running, growling at each other,
in contest over their performance.
Then the men, not so much their muted voices
as the rustling of hunting jackets
and the slap of shotguns against boots.

Blankets over pajamas, we'd stand shivering
watching the light snow whitewashing the barns,
covering the root cellar. Covering us.
We pretended not to notice
the men circling their trophies,
the talk increasing, and the laughter.
It was worth getting up for;
worth being part of the kill.

Deft, I would call it now,
the way the men handled the game,
a few rabbits, a few squirrels
strung like coon-skin caps from the clothesline
little heads tied with string to the wire,
men's knives glinting here and there
in the early light.

No malice. Just quick and even skill,
slitting the lifeless bodies from neck to groin,
peeling back the coat in one piece
ready for the next wearer.

Most days, I do not remember
December mornings from childhood.
Most days, I do not think of rabbit stew
or how squirrel tastes, roasted or fried.
But when a feast comes, when joy startles
the heart even for a moment,
a faint image reappears,
a few drops of red across a thin gray snow
and a feeble steam, rising.

In Search of the Phoenix

On blizzard days, we children sat before
The fire, returning chiefs who'd conquered, then
Conspired, to warm our alabaster toes,
Our frozen fingers back to ache again.

Before the darkness fell, the rite began.
My sister brought the butter from the crock.
My brother found the burlap sack that held
The mandarin kernels we would try to pop.

And when we took our offering to the gods,
Bright flames became the wings on which we flew.
Five hundred years, a thousand twilight dreams
Could not describe the ecstasies we knew.

We'd learned that rusty metal could not make
Field corn yield more than ashen bitter fare.
But we were sure that if we wished enough,
We could retain the magic in the air.

So now when snowstorms swirl, we sit
Before the fire to talk of battle clashes.
We're teacher, doctor, lawyer—yet still chiefs,
Who never will forget the taste of ashes.

First Kiss

What remains is colored by half a century,
by the lay of flat land in other school yards,
by the slant of light against other walls.

It must have been winter.
No colors, just dust and sharp shadows.

At five years old, I knew his face,
the conspiracies of his butterscotch eyes,
his body, round enough to put me at my ease.

It was not the kiss,
just the surprise of it,

the secret and breathless skirting
of the corner, the hiding just inside
the shadows, and no one noticing.

Since that moment,
I am spoiled for life.

I have counted days, turning each
in my hand at night like a globe,
searching, before letting it rest.

But something is always wanting.
I am forever waiting

for a subtle stirring of the heart,
for a sudden breathlessness,
for another first kiss.

The Riddle Song

Axle rhythms on the car's fragile shell
and I am a girl again, watching time
through a crack in the floorboard
run under me into the dark,
my lips still stinging—a mystery—
from the kiss of cold marble.

On the floormat, smooth as the inside of an egg,
the moon scatters patchwork. I see my friend,
her small face framed by a quilt,
the rough hewn bed gigantic around her.
"The heart had grown too big," they said,
"had cracked the worn ribs and burst."

I remember the Holy Ghost waiting there
in a black leather box, waiting
and swaying in the balsam house dangling
from a wire, from a pole at the top of the hill
swaying and stirring the dry grasses,
shadow puppets tumbling into the red dusk.

Dear, foetal figure in your car cradle,
one wet cheek to the frozen stars,
begin your rocking, your tapping
on the dark cave. First, the rhythm,
then metering of the memories,
and, at last, the lullaby.

Quoting Melville

Ten years I have carried this picture;
a yellow school bus in the morning mist,
windows steamy from its recent occupants,
finger-painted sites in every opaque frame.

That day, one teacher, thirty students
Rode, like warriors on their mounts,
shouting marching songs into the early leaves.
(*What like a bullet can undeceive?*)

You were sixteen.

Another First Manassas, another Second,
and no one can name the dust that covers you.
Most boundaries are not clearly defined.
A sniper's bullet, your picture on the front page,

and only one image can comfort me;
a yellow school bus in the morning mist,
each window witnessing: those who had been there,
could never be content in any fog bound world.

Lise-Lise

Some Samson stood and watched
her face turn red. He did not know
she had been planning for some months
to find a feat quite equal to her strength.

The chin that rested on her chest
showed signs of sturdiness
and every movement of her eyes
revealed the time had come
for her to pit her wit and will
against the daring task
that unknown ions had required.

She steeled her mouth
and strengthened, bit by bit, her spine
until she sat quite perpendicular to the floor
and felt, at last, the flood of fierce freedom.

Gianna's First Job

It must have had something to do with the river,
coming as it does from the place of my parents,
flowing swift and burnished
past River Bend Park after the rains.

Straight through the windows of the visitor's center,
and on the other side, the river charged—
a landscape framed and colored
in Rembrandt richness out of another century.

When my daughter had asked me for a ride,
I had almost said, "The park is close
enough for you to walk." But something
about her eyes had told me different.

Sitting together there in the car, we watched
leaves swirling about us like a surprise of snow.
"You'll do fine," I ventured, fourteen years of promise
settling into a moment which will never disappear.

She paused, as if to store my words for courage.
Then, blond hair swinging around, eyes straight ahead,
 "Bye, Mom," she said. And sprinted.
Another second, and she had disappeared

behind large wooden doors and into the future.
The river through the windows was the same,
except, that is, for a single glint of gold
and a loud pulsing sound which may have been my heart.

Starmaker

(After Visiting the Hayden Planetarium,
American Museum of Natural History, New York City)

"I will make stars! Hundreds of them
to fill our party's night sky," she proclaimed.
She fashioned the first few precisely,
their white points extending

at perfect angles, in straight lines
from their pentagonal centers.
At last, she thought, *I will begin*
to understand the nature of the universe.

As her momentum increased,
the points began to stretch.
With no warning, they were curving,
bending, abandoning their linear paths.

Soon, her joy came from deviation.
Maybe the Creator has a more various mind,
she mused, *a spastic hand,*
or some funny sense of humor in between.

She imitated Matisse, his dancers' adagio.
An attitude derrière here, a plié there,
an entrechat for good measure.
Cutting stars had become her domain.

How could she make flat paper
accept another dimension?
How far could she go
before she had gone too far?

After she had finished the first hundred, or so,
she began to hear music, a violin,
an oboe, a flute, one instrument at a time.
Then a whole orchestra warming up.

Stars started pirouetting,
rendering arabesques,
risking pas de deux.
The ballet had begun.

She was the princess, sur la pointe,
leaping through air. She could not contain
her glee. Stars were swirling around her-
green, red, blue, her private fireworks.

She became the Waking Beauty,
spinning out into space,
past a million trillion stars, past nebulae,
the Milky Way, the Black Hole,

a starmaker, trading her known world
for the enormity of the universe.

About the Author:

When Fay Picardi is not writing poetry about her childhood in Appalachia, she is traveling in France to practice her almost defunct French and in Italy where she is doing research on a novel at the Uffizi library and the Biblioteca Nazionale in Florence. Twice she has been a resident at the Atlantic Center for the Arts. Her poems have appeared in literary journals in the United States and Britain. Currently, she is working on two other chapbooks and a novel about Botticelli's model, Simonetta Vespucci. Fay has two daughters, three grandchildren, and lives in Grant, Florida with her husband. And, yes, Virginia, there is a town named Christmas.

Author's Notes:

I would like to recognize the very large part two excellent poets have played in my development over the years. Hillary Tham was for many years during her lifetime, my very good friend and mentor. She inspired and motivated me. I will always cherish the part she played in my life and work. Anthony Hecht, twice Poet Laureate of the United States, was my teacher and mentor at Atlantic Center for the Arts, and remained my friend until his death in 2004.

My special thanks to my husband, John Picardi, for his support, and to Kathy Garvey for her help in preparing this manuscript for publication. I would also like to thank my other colleagues at the Burnt Umber Press, Denette Schweikert and Cindy Michaud, for encouraging and supporting me in the publication of this chapbook.

9822430R0003

Made in the USA
Charleston, SC
16 October 2011